DON'T FORGET THE DUCT TAPE

D0011794

DON'T FORGET THE DUCT TAPE

Tips and Tricks for Repairing Outdoor Gear

Kristin Hostetter

 THE MOUNTAINEERS BOOKS

Published by
The Mountaineers Books
1001 SW Klickitat Way, Suite 201
Seattle, WA 98134

Published simultaneously in Great Britain by Cordee, 3a DeMontfort Street, Leicester, England, LE1 7HD

Manufactured in Canada

Acquisitions Editor: Laura Drury
Project Editor: Laura Drury
Copyeditor: Kris Fulsaas
Cover and Book Design: Ani Rucki
Layout: Peggy Egerdahl
Illustrations: Moore Creative Designs
Cover Illustration: Ani Rucki

Library of Congress Cataloging-in-Publication Data
Hostetter, Kristin.
   Don't forget the duct tape / Kristin Hostetter.
       p. cm. -- (Don't series)
Includes bibliographical references and index.
   ISBN 0-89886-906-4
   1. Outdoor recreation--Equipment and supplies--Maintenance and repair. I. Title.
   GV191.76.H67 2003
   796.5--dc21
                                            2003008323

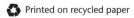 Printed on recycled paper

For Charlie and Joey

Contents

Acknowledgments

I am qualified to write this book only because I have spent time with some very wise outdoorspeople over the years. I am lucky to have shared many backcountry nights with my friends and colleagues from *Backpacker* magazine, especially Jonathan Dorn, Annette McGivney, and John Harlin. In addition to providing excellent company, they have shared many tricks of the trade, for which I am very grateful.

Thank you to Tom Shealey and John Viehman for hiring an inexperienced yet enthusiastic whippersnapper, fresh out of grad school, and showing me the ropes. I will always be grateful for the doors you helped me open.

Thank you to all my friends in the outdoor industry who have supported me, tormented me when they received a bad review, and taught me so much about outdoor equipment. You know who you are.

A special thanks to my friend Annie Getchell, the first lady of gear repair. Each day I spend with Annie, both in and out of the wilds, is a lesson in something—fixing a grumpy stove, painting a sun-bleached moose antler, cooking a sumptuous meal, or telling a story. Her excellent book, *The Essential Outdoor Gear Manual* (Ragged Mountain Press, 1995), goes into far more detail than this book can and also covers such topics as paddling, climbing, skiing, and gear-buying.

Last, thank you to my husband, Shaun, who has sacrificed lots of his precious basement space for my gear collection and who shares my passion for all things outdoors.

Introduction

Glorious views. Peaceful gurgles of a brook. Happy chirpings of wild birds. Air so fresh that it cleanses to the core. The contented pride you get after a long day's hike. These are just some of the things we enjoy about camping and hiking.

But there is another, less obvious aspect of living in the wild that brings great satisfaction: complete independence from the civilized world. There is something deeply gratifying in knowing that you have the ability to carry everything you need to survive and prosper in a nylon sack strapped to your back. The happiest campers are the ones who strip away all the distractions and extraneous clutter of everyday life and make do with what is on hand. The first time you remedy a leak in your tent, fashion a new strap for your backpack, or nurse a cranky stove back to life, you experience a sort of epiphany: you are truly self-sufficient, a regular Grizzly Adams.

That is the philosophical, romantic reason for this book.

Of course, there are other, more practical ones. You will save a bundle of money if you learn to maintain and fix damaged gear rather than replace it. You will do the environment a great service if you keep your old gear working smoothly rather than banishing it to the landfills. And perhaps the most important reason of all: you will enjoy your time spent in the wild if your equipment does not fail.

The goal of this book is to provide you with all the information and resources needed to care for and repair every item in your backpack—including the pack itself!

BACKPACKER'S REPAIR KITS

So what, you may ask, does it take to become an outdoor fix-it guru? Well, for starters, a good repair kit. Consider it your toolbox, a first-aid kit for your gear. A number of companies make and package basic gear-repair kits that are available at most outdoor shops.

You will want to weed out some items and include some additional ones, based on your own gear. You will want to change some of the contents, depending on the different types of trips you take. For instance, overnight and front-country trips do not require as deep a kit as a weeklong backcountry ramble. Some items you will not need to pack into the field, but you will want them at home for regular care and maintenance plus more elaborate repairs. The lists provided here are a good place to start.

Once your repair kit is assembled, it will weigh about a pound or two. All the contents can be packed in a sturdy zippered pouch, stuff sack, or gallon-size, freezer-weight zipper-lock plastic bag.

When packing for your next backpacking trip, you might be tempted to jettison your repair kit along with your portable coffee-bean grinder and cushy camp chair. But don't! Hopefully you will not need a repair kit at all, but if your boot sole starts flapping and you don't have the goods to fix it, your whole trip will be ruined. Don't forget: a good repair kit is worth its weight in gorp.

Backpacking Repair-Kit Checklist

✔ good-quality duct tape
✔ assortment of fabric swatches (mosquito netting and lightweight ripstop nylon for tent repairs, pack cloth for garment and bag repairs, heavier Cordura for pack repairs)
✔ assortment of plastic buckles for pack repairs
✔ assortment of needles and safety pins (packed inside a 35mm film canister for safety)

✔ aluminum pole-repair sleeve
✔ adhesive/seam sealer such as Seam Grip
✔ 5–10 feet of nylon parachute cord
✔ dental floss
✔ assortment of threads (cotton, cotton/polyester, nylon)
✔ a few heavy-duty rubber bands
✔ a lightweight multitool, preferably one that includes small pliers and scissors
✔ extra clevis pins for an external frame pack (if you carry one)

At-Home Repair-Kit Checklist

✔ mild soap (not detergent) such as Ivory Flakes
✔ assortment of plastic-bristled brushes
✔ toothbrush
✔ irrigation syringe (for seam sealing)
✔ seam sealer
✔ boot goop (waterproofing agent and conditioner)
✔ assortment of waterproofing agents for tent, rain gear, etc.
✔ pliers
✔ more duct tape (of course!)

Duct Tape Tip

Wrap a generous amount of duct tape around the middle of a trekking pole, hiking staff, or flashlight, and leave the bulky roll at home.

WHY DUCT TAPE RULES

Duct tape is the single most useful repair tool you can carry on a backpacking trip, bar none. The best tape to use: standard-grade (9mm), slick, silver fabric tape (no plastic). Opt for the stickiest tape that pulls off the roll with the most resistance, so it will not peel off should it become wet.

What else can fix pack, boots, tent, clothes, stove, filter, pad, sunglasses, stuff sack, and your very own feet (see the next section)? If you need convincing that duct tape is a worthwhile addition to your backpack, below are a few ingenious ways you might use it on your next hiking/camping trip.

Note: Many more duct tape ideas are scattered throughout the book—look for the Duct Tape Tip sidebars.

✔ Got a gash on your rain jacket or backpack? Tape it up.

✔ Forgot your sunglasses leash? Your spoon? You can construct just about anything with a little imagination and a bit of duct tape.

✔ Sore hips? If your pack's hip belt starts chaffing during a trip, tape a tee shirt or some other piece of soft clothing to each pad of the hip belt.

✔ Got binding blues? Skiers and snowshoers simply must carry a good supply of duct tape, which can be a lifesaver in the case of a blown binding or a bent or broken pole.

✔ Close encounter with a cactus? Gently press a piece of duct tape to the spine-covered body part and pull the spines out with one fell swoop.

Duct Taping Blisters

Many people swear by duct tape for fixing foot woes, but unlike most other blister products, duct tape is not a cushy, comfy, tender-loving blister swaddler. Know how to use it properly so it does not exacerbate the damage.

✔   Try taping *over* socks in problem areas or applying
     tape to pesky seams inside your boots.

✔   Instead of applying sticky duct tape directly to a sore
     or blistered area, place a single layer of toilet paper
     over the skin, then apply the tape. Another solution
     is to use a second piece of duct tape—sticky side to
     sticky side, so that the smooth part is against the skin.

✔   For additional stickiness, apply tincture of benzoin to
     the skin around the perimeter of your tape job.

CHAPTER 1.

Fabric

IMAGINE THIS:

The sun is finally shining after a few days of monsoonlike weather. You declare a rest day and spread all your gear out in the strong August sun to dry. Unfortunately, you unfurled your down sleeping bag a bit too close to a thorny blackberry bush, and now there is a 2-inch gash spewing precious feathers over your campsite like snow. Are you doomed to watch as your cozy bag shrivels into a useless sack of nylon, or are you equipped with the supplies and skills for making a life-saving patch?

For the most part, the modern outdoorsperson uses gear and clothing made of lightweight synthetic fabrics. Ninety-five percent of your outdoor wardrobe is, or should be, made of some sort of synthetic material. Fleece, lightweight ripstop nylon, pack cloth, and heavier Cordura are some of the fabrics used for outdoor gear and clothing. Synthetics are ideal for outdoor use because they are rugged, they dry quickly, and they do not absorb water like natural fibers such as cotton and wool do. They are low maintenance to boot.

Shelter from the elements is your number one concern in the backcountry and, arguably, the most sinister element you will have to contend with is rain. This is why it is so important that your gear and clothing use waterproof fabrics. Most outdoor fabrics are either coated (most often found on tents) or laminated to a waterproof/breathable membrane (most often found on rain jackets and pants). The magic ingredient that makes water bead up and roll off all waterproof fabrics is called a DWR (durable, water-repellent) treatment.

Quality Counts

The thick, heavy, yellow slicker material used for our childhood rain jackets really has no place in the wilds because the stuff, although perfectly waterproof, has zero breathability. If you tried hiking in a nonbreathable rain suit or sleeping in a nonbreathable tent, you would quickly be soaked not from the rain, but from your own perspiration.

It is also important that waterproof gear has sealed seams. Luckily for us, most raingear seams are factory-taped these days. You can see the outline of seam taping through the outside of the fabric. If your raingear has any seams that are not taped (fig. 1-1b), apply a seam sealer, just as you would on a tent (see chapter 5, Tents).

CARING FOR SYNTHETIC FABRICS

The most common problem with fleeces and other synthetic fabrics is pilling. Over time, pilling is pretty much inevitable, but rest assured that it will not affect the performance of the fabric. If you want to groom your fleece jacket to make it look a bit fresher, brush the fabric with a pumice stone (the type used to remove calluses on feet works just fine) or a plastic-bristled kitchen brush.

Over time, the Velcro on all your gear will wind up caked with little fuzz balls that prevent it from doing its job. There are two sides to Velcro: the hook (scratchy) side and the loop (fuzzy) side. Clean the hook side by scraping out debris with a fine-toothed comb. Put the loop side under the faucet and scrub it with an old toothbrush.

Fig. 1-1. Seams

a) taped seam

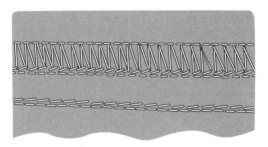

b) untaped seam

CLEANING SYNTHETIC FABRICS

Keep the fabrics of your gear clean. First rule: before laundering, always read the label. As a general rule of thumb, synthetics can be washed in your home laundry machine using the gentle cycle, cold water, and mild soap. Your outdoor shop may carry some soaps made specifically for raingear; these work well, but tend to be pricey.

An Ounce of Prevention: Button Up!

Before washing outdoor gear, make sure all zippers are zipped, snaps are snapped, and—this is *important*—Velcro is closed. This prevents the wear and tear of abrasion on the fabric.

The best way to wash your raingear is in a front-loading commercial washer (found at a Laundromat) because they lack the spindle agitators that can be rough on your gear. Use cold water, the gentle cycle, and a mild laundry soap.

Because your synthetics will be virtually dry after undergoing the spin cycle of your washer, there is no need to throw them in the dryer. Just hang them up for a half hour or so and they are ready for action. If you do want to put synthetics in your clothes dryer, again, read the label. As a general rule, synthetics can be dried in your dryer using the gentle/delicate setting and low/no heat.

REVIVING WATERPROOF FABRICS

You will spend a bundle on your waterproof fabrics, but the time will come when your jacket or tent fly seems to be absorbing rain rather than repelling it. This is because the outer fabric's DWR treatment has worn off. Just like a good wax job on your car, this coating wears off over time, leaving you feeling wet even if no rain has actually penetrated the fabric.

When this happens, do not immediately go storming off to the shop that sold it to you. There are some simple, inexpensive things you can do to revive your waterproof gear if it starts to seep.

Wash it. Over time, dirt and things like campfire smoke get into the fabric and prevent the DWR treatment from doing its job. Some folks have gone years without washing their waterproof/breathable gear for fear that they will harm it. It may sound simple, but for the most part, occasional washing is a must. See "Cleaning Synthetic Fabrics" earlier in this chapter.

Machine-dry it. Machine-drying on a medium setting will reactivate the DWR coating that is left in the fabric, unless the manufacturer recommends otherwise. See "Cleaning Synthetic Fabrics."

Iron it. As strange as it may sound, carefully running a warm iron (on a low setting) over your waterproof garment brings even more of those DWR molecules to life. Before ironing, be sure to wipe down the iron to make sure it is clean.

Check the seams. If your seam tape is peeling or leaking, send it back to the manufacturer for repair. It's always under warrantee.

Reapply a DWR treatment. If you do all of the above steps and rain still does not bead up and run off your garment, it means your existing DWR treatment is all but gone and it is time to reapply a new one. There are a number of good DWR treatments on the market, available as either spray-on or wash-in; Table 1-1 lists the advantages and disadvantages of each.

For a spray-on treatment, hang the garment outdoors or in a well-ventilated place. Use long, uniform strokes and try to prevent drips. It is better to apply two light coats rather than one thick one.

For a wash-in treatment, prewash the garment. Fill the

drum of the washing machine with water, add the treatment, wait a few minutes, then add the garment and complete the wash cycle.

Table 1-1.

Comparing DWR Treatments

	Pros	Cons
Spray-on treatments	Tend to repel rain a bit better.	Tough to get a perfectly smooth, even coating.
Wash-in treatments	Easy and clean to apply, and you get a perfectly distributed coating.	One more load of laundry to do!

PATCHING SYNTHETIC FABRICS

The Perfect Patch

You do not need to be Martha Stewart in order to fix torn outdoor gear. All you need is a sturdy needle, the right sort of thread, and a swatch of fabric—preferably one similar in weight to the one you are repairing—big enough to cover the damaged area. Here is a step-by-step guide to patching just about anything:

1. Using scissors, cut a rounded patch of fabric bigger than the hole or damaged area by about 1 inch on all sides.
2. Turn the item inside out and lay the patch in place. Avoid pinning it in place because this can cause more damage to the fabric—especially waterproof ones.
3. Make small, tightly spaced overhand stitches (see the next section) around the patch and tie it off securely on the back.
4. Seam-seal around the stitch lines if necessary (fig. 1-2).

Fig. 1-2. Patching

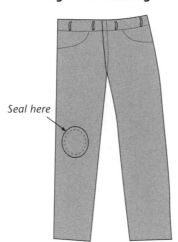

Seal here

Stitches You Should Know

Overhand stitch. This is perfect for patching holes in sleeping bag shells, clothing, or tent walls. Simply loop the needle through the fabric layers so that the stitches make little parallel slanting lines (fig. 1-3a). This is the simplest of stitches—even if you have ten thumbs.

Backstitch. This is ideal for repairing seam tears or patching when strength is more an issue. You reinforce each stitch by doubling back over it (fig. 1-3b).

Bar tack. This is great for fixing blown pack straps or mending pocket tears. Make three to five long stitches running parallel to the tear. Then make a zillion small, tight overhand stitches across the long ones to close the gap. Augment the repair with tiny bar stitches at either end, so that the finished work resembles a capital "I" (fig. 1-3c).

Fig. 1-3. Basic Stitches

a) overhand stitch

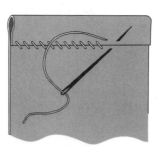

b) backstitch

c) bar tack

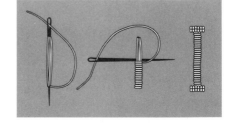

Repairing Mosquito Netting

There is nothing more annoying than an elusive mosquito making kamikaze runs at your ears all night long. That is why it pays to know what to do if the mosquito netting on your tent, garment, or hat gets a gash.

Large tears or holes can be patched using the swatch of mosquito netting from your repair kit and a simple overhand stitch (see the preceding section). If the hole is smaller than 1 inch in diameter, try this handy technique:

1. Place a piece of paper (the table of contents from your novel will do just fine) over the hole (either side of the fabric is fine) and secure it with duct tape.

2. Turn the fabric over and smear a generous amount of Seam Grip over the paper-backed hole, smoothing it into a sheet.

3. After the Seam Grip has cured completely (ideally, 48 hours), peel off the tape and paper, leaving the Seam Grip filling the hole. **Note:** Do not pack the tent, garment, or hat unless the Seam Grip is totally dry—you could create a massive knot of fabric and glue that would be nearly impossible to fix in the field.

Duct Tape Tip

Resist the urge to make a quick duct-tape patch on fabric unless you absolutely have to. The tape will eventually peel away and leave a sticky residue on the fabric, which makes permanent repairs more difficult. Instead, retire to your tent a little early and practice your sewing skills. In the long run, you will be much happier—and so will your gear.

CHAPTER 2.

Zippers

IMAGINE THIS:
You are 20 miles from the nearest trailhead when your pack explodes all over the pine needles. Spontaneous combustion? Not quite. The U-shaped zipper on your pack's front panel finally succumbed to the stresses of overload and physical abuse. Will a whole lot of luck and duct tape put your pack back together again? Or do you know how to handle a zipper emergency?

Zippers adorn nearly every piece of soft gear that accompanies you into the woods—clothes, tent, bag, pack. There are two basic kinds of zippers: coiled and toothed.

Most of the zippers you'll find on outdoor gear are coil zippers, made from tiny loops or coils sewn into the zipper tape fabric. The beauty of coil zips is that they are often self-healing, meaning that when a crimp in one of the coils happens, all you do is pass the slider (the tab you grab and slide up and down) back and forth, and the coils straighten themselves out.

Toothed zippers—with their interlocking wedge-shaped teeth—are generally less desirable than coil zips because once a tooth breaks, there is nothing you can do short of replacing the whole zipper.

Quality Counts
When it comes to zippers, beefier is better. Also, opt for coil zippers over toothed zippers. Coils are much easier to repair.

The ubiquitous zipper is a wonderful invention. The problem is, they tend to break—so it pays to know how to fix them. If you do not know what to do, a zapped zipper can be a major disaster, especially if the nighttime temperature has dropped like an anchor and your tent door is flapping in the breeze. This chapter teaches you how to fix the four most common zipper failures—crushed coils, broken teeth, a worn slider, and a broken pull—and to care for your zippers so these things never happen in the first place.

An Ounce of Prevention: Do Not Yank!

Pulling on a zipper to unstick it only mangles the slider (see Repairing a Worn Slider) and causes more problems. Treat your zippers kindly and they will continue to work for you indefinitely.

CLEANING ZIPPERS

If your zippers seem balky, it may be because grit is living inside the teeth or coils. Using a damp toothbrush, scrub the zipper on both sides, then let it air dry. Avoid lubricating it with oil or silicone spray, as this just attracts more dirt.

REPAIRING CRUSHED OR DAMAGED COILS

Sometimes those coils get crushed beyond the point of self-healing. If this happens, try to reshape the coils by inserting a sewing needle or straightened safety pin underneath one coil at a time and gently pulling the coil upward and back into shape (fig. 2-1). If the coils look rough or full of burrs, try gently filing them smooth with an emery board.

Figure 2-1. Coil Zipper

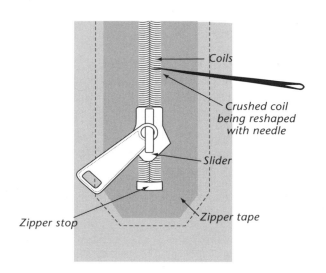

Coils

Crushed coil
being reshaped
with needle

Slider

Zipper stop

Zipper tape

REPAIRING A BROKEN ZIPPER TOOTH

If you are in the field and need that broken zipper to function
till the end of your trip, get out your needle and thread and
sew the zipper shut where the tooth is missing (fig. 2-2). At the
very least, your zipper will work up to that point, and you can
replace it with a proper coil zipper when you get back home.

REPAIRING A WORN SLIDER

You are strolling down the trail when a chilly gust of wind re-
minds you to zip up your jacket. When you do, the zipper in-
explicably pops open in the middle. This is the symptom of
the most common zipper ailment: a worn slider. When a slider

Figure 2-2. Toothed Zipper

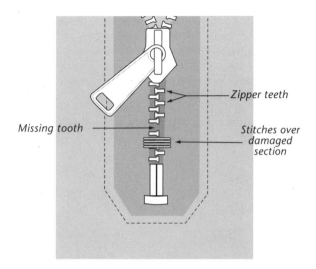

Zipper teeth

Missing tooth

Stitches over damaged section

gets worn, its shape changes slightly, which prohibits it from properly aligning the two sides of the zipper.

How does a slider wear out? Regular, proper use usually is not enough to damage a good slider. But if dirt or grit finds its way inside or along the coils themselves, the damage can be quick and lethal. Even more common is general abuse. How many times have you gotten frustrated with your zipper, then yanked and yanked and yanked on it until it finally surrendered? Or when a bit of fabric gets jammed, do you jerk on the zipper and try to strong-arm it into submission? Well, that is the sort of thing that hurts zippers most.

The good news is that many sliders can be repaired using

only a small set of pliers—the type found on many pocket tools. In the case of the fabric getting caught in the zipper, use your pliers to gently pull the fabric out. In the case of a worn, tired, or misshapen slider, open the zipper all the way up. Next, use your pliers to *very* gently pinch one of the two openings a little more closed (fig. 2-3). Then pinch the other side, using equal pressure. Try the zipper. Repeat this gradual pinching process until the slider is sufficiently tightened and your zipper stays zipped.

Figure 2-3. Repairing a Worn Slider

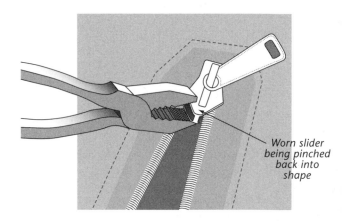

Worn slider
being pinched
back into
shape

REPAIRING A BROKEN, LOST, OR INADEQUATE ZIPPER PULL

It happens all the time. The little grab-tab on the end of the zipper either disappears or is simply so small that you need a set of tweezers to find it. If this happens, simply remove the old tab and attach a new and improved one. You are limited

Figure 2-4. Duct Tape Puller

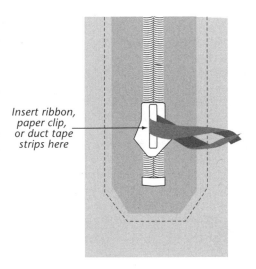

Insert ribbon, paper clip, or duct tape strips here

only by your imagination. Use ribbon, cord, a paper clip, a whistle, or a thermometer (fig. 2-4). Generally speaking, the bigger the pull the better, especially if it is a zipper you intend to use while wearing gloves or mittens.

Duct Tape Tip
Make a sturdy zipper pull by threading a thin strip of duct tape through the slider, then wrapping the tails with more duct-tape strips.

CHAPTER 3.

Boots

IMAGINE THIS:
You spent all day slogging across streams and through puddles and now your boots are sodden, cold, leather foot-prisons. You snuggle up to a crackling fire, doff your boots, and place them near the heat to dry out. The next morning your boots are cozy and dry, but also a full size smaller! After a mile on the trail, the heat-shrunken leather has chafed your heels into oozing craters of flesh. Could you have spared yourself this agony and still walked away with dry feet?

A good pair of boots should last for many years, provided that you care for them properly. Most boot problems happen over time, so regular inspection of and prompt attention to the soles, seams, and materials can save you from blowing something out in the field.

Quality Counts

If you often find yourself in wet conditions, you will do well to invest in Gore-Tex hiking boots (up to $50 more). Sure, they may make your feet sweat a bit more, and you still have to treat the leather portions, but unless water spills over the boot tops, your feet will not get wet in Gore-Tex boots. Period.

BREAKING IN NEW BOOTS

When you invest in a new pair of boots, you immediately want to take them on a hike, just like when you get a new car and cannot wait for that first drive. But you would be wise to resist that temptation and give yourself ample time to break in new boots. The heavier and stiffer the boots, the more break-in time they will need, but even the lightest-weight hiking boots deserve a few days of test runs before they hit the trail.

The best tool for breaking in new boots is one we never seem to have: time. The moment you get home from the store, put your new boots on and wear them around the house for a few days. This will give you time to be sure you have made the right decision without gunking up the boots so badly that the store will not take them back. (Most good stores will let you return the boots after a few days, as long as they are still clean and have not been worn outside.)

Once you are satisfied that you have made the right choice, start wearing your boots on errands around town—walking the dog, to the market, etc. Wear them to the office if you can—the more wear time the better. After a few days, it is safe to start taking them on day hikes. Then you can gradually build up to longer trips.

Sometimes, though, we do not have the luxury of time, so below are a few tips that will help you speed up the process. These tips are geared mostly toward unruly leather boots. For lightweight fabric–leather boots, you should not have to resort to any of these methods.

The Full Wetting

Wear the boots down to your favorite creek. Walk into the creek until water pours over the top and into your boots. Stand there until the boots are thoroughly soaked—inside and out. If it is chilly, you may want to wear Gore-Tex socks over your hiking socks to keep your feet dry. Then go for a long hike and wear the boots until they dry. Once dry, they will have magically molded to your feet and all their quirky contours.

Leather Softeners

A thin application of mink oil or any other oil-based leather treatment softens the leather so that it can more easily mold to your feet. On lighter-weight boots, though, beware. Oversoftening can lead to boots that have little or no support.

Rubbing Bar

If there is a specific area that keeps bothering you, such as near your piggy toe or at the base of your big toe, try this method. First, soften the area with a bit of mink oil. Then, using a smooth, blunt, hard object, like the end of your (closed) pocketknife or the end of a broomstick, repeatedly rub the offending area into submission. In essence, you are creating a pocket of space for that part of your foot.

WATERPROOFING LEATHER BOOTS

Few things in outdoor life are more depressing than cold, wet, pruney feet. Therefore, it is hard to overstate the importance of waterproofing your boots. By applying a waterproofer properly and in a timely manner, you not only help to keep your feet dry and warm, you are also feeding and nurturing the leather, which extends its life span and performance.

The key to maintaining the health of your boots' leather is to try to keep it at an equilibrium. Overly wet leather is prone to tearing; overly dry leather is prone to cracking. By applying the right stuff at the right time, you keep the leather supple, healthy, and strong.

What is the right stuff? There are loads of good waterproofers out there, all tailored to work with different types of leather and materials. Talk to a knowledgeable salesperson about what type will work best with the boots you have. Avoid using mink oil or any other type of oil that will oversoften most backpacking and hiking boots. (**Note:** If your intent is to simply soften stiff, unyielding leather, a dab of mink oil may help.)

Whichever treatment you use, be sure to follow the instructions carefully. Two or three thin coats are better than one thick, gloppy one. Also, contrary to some old-timers' opinions, you should never warm your boots in the oven prior to treatment—unless you want the toes to curl up like clown shoes and the glue to melt all over the place.

When is the right time to treat your boots? Depending on the amount of wear they get, boots will need treating about one to three times a year, or whenever the leather starts to lighten in color and look dry and thirsty.

A few more treatment tips:

✔   Before you start working, take out the laces and pull out the tongue. Be sure to apply the boot goop to all the little nooks and crannies—such as in the tongue gussets and around each eyelet.

✔   After the boot goop has had ample cure time, buff the boots with a boot brush. This is not to make them look nattier, though they surely will, but to smooth and harden the finish. If, after a day or so, your boots still feel tacky or there is a visible waxy buildup, you may have been overly generous with your goop. Wipe off the excess and buff until they are smooth.

✔   For fabric-leather boots with multiple seams, seal the seams with an irrigation syringe *before* you waterproof the boots. Purchase a can of spray-on fabric water treatment for the fabric portions of the boots. The leather can be treated as discussed above, but the fabric requires a different sort of concoction.

CARING FOR YOUR BOOTS

When you reach the car after a wet, mucky hike, avoid the temptation to stuff your poor, hardworking boots into a plastic bag and toss it into a corner of the basement. A week later, when you open that bag, you will find a science project—colonies of mold and mildew in the shape of a boot.

An Ounce of Prevention: Dry Slowly

Never dry wet boots near a fire or other heat source, unless you *want* to destroy them, shrink them, or both. The best way to dry boots is slowly but surely. Remove the insoles and laces. Open the boots up as much as possible for maximum airflow. Insert newspaper. If you are in the field, try chemical heating packs/handwarmers.

Find yourself a good local cobbler who has experience with hiking boots to assist you with major repairs. Especially if your boots are expensive, it is wise to leave big jobs to the pros. That said, there are some things you should know about dealing with problems that occur while you are out on the trail.

REPAIRING PEELING SOLES

If your boots are old-school Norwegian-welted boots (they have a visible line of stitching where sole meets leather), do not try to repair any of the stitching yourself—trust them to a cobbler. However, most boots these days have soles that are glued, rather than stitched, to the upper, and with a bit of effort, you can probably do a pretty good repair job on your own.

If your boot sole starts flapping in the field, your only real choice is to duct tape it thoroughly and hope it holds till you make it home. Once you and the boot are home, here is an easy six-step procedure to fix the problem.

Fig. 3-1. Fixing a Peeling Boot Sole

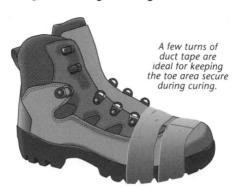

A few turns of duct tape are ideal for keeping the toe area secure during curing.

1. Start by making sure the boot is clean. Wash it with soap and water and let it dry completely before proceeding. Then wipe down the area in question with alcohol.
2. Cram the boot cavity with socks or newspaper. This ensures that the boot retains its proper shape under the pressure you are about to exert.
3. Using a good contact cement designed for shoe repair (Shoe Goo or Barge are two examples), smear the leather and the sole where the two were once—and will be again!—joined. Wait until the cement is almost dry but still tacky.
4. Next, carefully press the sole into place on the upper. Use a steady hand and be sure to mate the two pieces accurately; once they touch, the cemented parts are just that—cemented.
5. Dig a C-clamp from your toolbox and use it to pinch the boot tightly together at the appropriate place. Let the boot rest until the cement is totally, completely, thoroughly, 100 percent dry.

6. Last, inject seam sealer into the joint with an irrigation syringe.

Duct Tape Tip
When regluing a boot sole, a few turns of duct tape can keep the toe area secure while the glue dries. (fig.3-1)

FIXING SMALL TEARS AND HOLES

Small gashes and tiny puncture holes in leather can be remedied by using a bit of adhesive. Seam Grip will work in a pinch, but boots are best patched using a urethane specifically designed for the task, such as Freesole. Just smooth a clump of the sticky stuff into the cleaned and prepped wound, then let it rest until thoroughly cured. Larger openings will require the services of a cobbler.

Chapter 4.

Packs

> **IMAGINE THIS:**
> *After an extravagant lunch of salami and Swiss cheese bagels, you dread donning your gigantic pack for the 5-mile march to tonight's camp. You take a deep breath, grab a shoulder strap, and brace yourself for the 50-pound load. Pop! The webbing explodes from the pack bag, leaving you with a dangling strap and a small gaping hole, neither of which will do, considering there is no wheelbarrow handy to ferry your busted pack down the trail. Do you sit down on a rock and wait for the search and rescue crew? Or do you have what it takes to fix the fix you are in?*

Backpacks come in two basic constructions: external frame and internal frame. External frame packs are kind of like Volkswagen Beetles: they were all the rage back in the '60s and '70s, then they all but died out of fashion, and now they have been updated and revamped with new materials and have crept back into vogue. Internal frame packs still greatly outnumber externals, but wise backpackers know that externals are the real workhorses of the pack world. Externals fall into two categories—old-school aluminum frames and new plastic frames.

CARING FOR YOUR PACK
There are a few things you should know about caring for your pack. Here are some tips to ensure your pack a longer life.

At home, inspect the inside seams of the pack. If any fabric edges are fraying, trim them neatly with scissors so they do not snag in the pack's zippers.

Quality Counts

Because your pack will often be filled to the gills with heavy gear, its seams need to be burly enough to handle the pressure. Check the pack's innards for tight, finished seams and beware of loose, fraying ends or single stitching. And although supercushy foam in the pack's waist belt and shoulder straps may sound like a good idea and feel good at first, it often turns into a pancake after a bit of use. Look for foam that is soft yet dense, so that it will not lose its integrity over the long haul.

When packing your pack, make sure sharp objects such as tent stakes, tent poles, and stoves are padded so they do not rub against the inside of your pack and cause a rip.

At rest breaks on the trail, instead of dropping your pack down with a thump, remember how much it cost, then set it down gently instead.

Keep your pack food-free. Make sure to remove any food crumbs from the pockets and recesses of your pack both in the field and for long-term storage at home. Little woodland critters think nothing of chewing a hole through nylon, even for a tiny cookie crumb.

CLEANING YOUR PACK

Granola crumbs, bug repellent, and plain old sweat are some of the things that can turn your pack into a grimy, stinky sack. You will probably need to wash your pack only every couple of seasons or so—unless a calamity such as a leaky fuel bottle happens (see An Ounce of Prevention: Double-Bag Liquids).

Fill a bucket with warm water and a bit of dissolved soap

An Ounce of Prevention: Pack Covers

Because of their multiple, complicated seams and rugged, porous fabrics, backpacks by themselves are rarely waterproof. There are a few exceptions: packs designed for boaters and canyoneers. To keep your backpack and all its contents dry, invest in a nylon pack cover and pop it on at the first sign of troubled skies. If your pack cover's waterproofing starts to get tired, it can be recoated just like a tent fly (see chapter 5, Tents).

(Ivory Flakes or a mild dishwashing soap will do). Using a vegetable brush, scrub every inch of the pack, inside and out, including all the corners, sweaty straps, zippers, and buckles. Give the whole pack a good, high-pressure rinse with a garden hose and hang it outside to air dry.

An Ounce of Prevention: Double-Bag Liquids

A leaky bottle of liquid—cooking oil, sticky beverages, sunscreen, and the like—can be a debacle, not only for all the gear in your pack but the pack itself. Double-bag bottles of liquids inside zipper-lock bags, then pack them far away from your food and clothes, preferably in their own side pocket.

REPAIRING PACK FRAMES

Pack disasters that do not involve zippers or fabrics are rare, but occasionally you will need to make field repairs on such things as the pack's frame. The good thing about external

Fig. 4-1. Spare Tension Buckle

Slot

This type is ideal for repairs because of the slot. No need for sewing

aluminum frames is that they most often bend before they break, giving you the opportunity to make the repair before a total blowout occurs. If an aluminum frame bends, try to gently bend it back, but you would be wise to make a precautionary splint so it does not break the next time you drop your pack.

In the case of a broken frame member on either an external- or internal-frame pack, all you need to do is fashion a makeshift splint. Your options for materials are limited only by your imagination: a tent stake, a cut-up aluminum can wrapped around the frame, or a sturdy stick all do the trick when secured around the bend or break with a healthy dose of duct tape.

REPAIRING PACK BUCKLES

For starters, always make sure your repair kit includes spare buckles that match those on your pack—especially the large hip-belt buckle, which is notorious for breaking first. Of course, your pack is still functional if this burly buckle breaks, but your shoulders will hate you for not being able to replace or fix it.

The second critical pack buckle that is prone to breaking is located on your pack straps—the tension buckles that allow you to cinch the shoulder straps tight and shift the weight around. If one of these breaks, you will have to cut the webbing, then sew it shut around a new buckle, unless you happen to have a spare that is designed for such purposes (fig. 4-1). These handy repair buckles have a slot on the second bar that allows you to simply slip the webbing loop right back into place.

REPAIRING PACK STRAPS

If the scenario described at the beginning of this chapter happens to you, no amount of duct tape will save you. Luckily, a dip into your well-stocked sewing kit and about 20 minutes of careful stitching are all that stand between you and happy

Fig. 4-2. Fixing a Strap Blowout

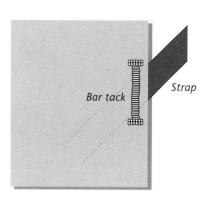

Bar tack

Strap

trails. Chances are, the strap blowout happened where the webbing strap attaches to the nylon of the pack bag, sandwiched between a side seam.

Turn the pack bag inside out and, from the outside, poke the orphaned strap back through the original opening. Using your largest needle and a strong polyester thread, fashion a sturdy bar tack (see Stitches You Should Know in chapter 1, Fabric) that reattaches the webbing to the two layers of fabric (fig. 4-2).

Duct Tape Tip

If the female (socket) side of your pack's hip-belt buckle cracks or breaks and you find yourself without a spare (shame!), you can hold it together with a few wraps of duct tape until you get back home.

CHAPTER 5.

Tents

IMAGINE THIS:
You are three days into a weeklong hike through a remote wilderness. While stopping for a rest break under gathering storm clouds, you gratefully ditch your overloaded pack. It lands with a thud and a loud snap. Upon inspection, you discover that one of the four tent poles that was strapped to the outside of your pack has snapped. Have you packed the necessary tools to repair the pole and guarantee a dry, comfortable night? Or will you be soggy and cold in a droopy tent?

This chapter covers all types and shapes of double-wall tents. Single-wall tents use delicate fabrics that really should be repaired by experts (see the appendix, Repair Facility Reference Guide, at the back of this book).

Quality Counts

When shopping for a new tent, be sure to set it up and stake it out tightly (most stores provide Velcro "carpet stakes") to be sure the tent is taut and tightly sewn together. You should be able to bounce a quarter off any given side of a well-made tent. This means the tent will send precipitation bouncing away from you when bad weather strikes.

PACKING YOUR TENT

There are two schools of thought on tent packing. "Rollers" meticulously lay out the tent, fold it neatly into thirds, then roll it up like a sleeping pad, and slip it into its sack. If you are the rolling type, just be sure to shift the fold line every now and then to avoid permanently creasing the fabric and possibly cracking any waterproof coating.

"Crammers" simply open the mouth of the stuff sack and start stuffing—first the fly, then the tent body, or vice versa. This method may go against your fervent desire to pamper your sizable investment, but most seasoned outdoorsfolk opt for cramming. It is so much faster and easier, especially if the stuff sack is on the smallish side.

An Ounce of Prevention: Double-Bag Your Stakes

Be sure to pack tent stakes in a small but rugged sack so there is no chance they will puncture or tear the delicate tent fabric in transit.

PREVENTING CONDENSATION

Oftentimes it is not an actual tent leak that gets you wet, but condensation buildup inside the tent—the result of you and your tentmates breathing all night. Some tents have well-placed windows and vents, and therefore are inherently better at battling condensation, but a few techniques will help you win the war in any tent.

Setup

First, be sure to set up your tent properly. This may seem obvious, but many people just shove the poles in their sleeves and call it good. For a supertaut pitch that will have water pinging off your rain fly, start by staking out each and every spot on your tent's floor to give you maximum interior space.

Then attach the fly and repeat the process, using all the available stake-out loops and guy lines. Install line tensioners, little aluminum or plastic figure-eight-like gadgets, on all your guy lines. These allow you to easily stake out a guy line, then tighten it without moving the stake (especially helpful on rocky ground where it is tough to find a secure position for stakes).

Placement

Try to pitch your tent on high ground, where you are more likely to catch a little breeze. If the wind is really howling, pitch the lowest side of the tent (often the foot end) into the wind to create a more aerodynamic shape. If the weather is still and steamy, pitch the biggest expanse of mesh (often the door) facing the wind.

Fig. 5-1. High-Low Venting, a.k.a. The Chimney Effect

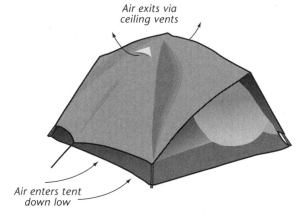

Air exits via ceiling vents

Air enters tent down low

Airflow

Once your tent is erected, use the windows and door(s) to achieve optimum airflow inside. Ideally, you want to create the chimney effect, where cool air comes into your tent from down low and has a place to exit up high (fig. 5-1). Play around with the zippers on the windows and door(s) to get the best high-low airflow.

CLEANING AND STORING YOUR TENT

A tent's number-one enemy is unchecked moisture. Tents can remain erect in the rain indefinitely with no damage, but if you pack a sodden tent into its stuff sack and leave it there for a day or two, it is doomed. It will become infested with mold and mildew that can weaken the waterproof coating and the fabric itself, plus leave your backwoods abode with a perpetual stink. The moral: Be sure to unpack a wet tent as soon as possible and set it up, preferably in a sunny, breezy place.

Eventually your tent will succumb to the griminess of outdoor living. Dead mosquitoes smeared against the interior walls, dried mud and spilled food on the floor, sand stuck in the zippers—these are all par for the course in the wilderness. At some point you will have to resort to soap and water.

You may be thinking . . . hey, it is made of fabric just like my raingear, so why not toss it in the washing machine and be done in a snap? Because tents—with their mosquito netting and special waterproof coatings—are too delicate for the likes of your washing machine. It does not take long to do the job right, and hand-washing gives you the chance to closely inspect every square inch of the tent for wear, tear, and downright damage.

Erect your tent on a grassy patch of yard. Dissolve a mild soap (such as Ivory Flakes) into a big bucket of water and start scrubbing with a large car wash-style sponge. Use a fingernail or vegetable brush on the webbing stake-out loops and zipper tracks. Finish with a good blast from the garden hose, then let your tent air-dry completely.

An Ounce of Prevention: UV Damage

It may sound like fun to leave your tent set up in the backyard for the kids to play in, but if you do, you cannot count on it to keep you warm and dry on your next camping trip. Prevention of ultraviolet (UV) damage is really all you can do, because there is no way to fix UV-damaged fabric, which is generally too weak to even patch. Normal use will not inflict UV damage to your tent, so don't worry about using it on a sunny, weeklong trip. If you have the option, choose a site that is at least partially shaded and do not leave the tent set up in the sun any longer than necessary.

POLES

Tent poles are the skeleton of your shelter. Just as you would be unable to function without your bones, your tent is hard-pressed to do its job of protecting you without its poles. With their bendy shapes that are perfectly sized for your particular tent, poles are almost impossible to improvise but are very easy to fix, provided you have the right stuff.

Quality Counts

Aluminum tent poles perform better than fiberglass ones, which are prone to splintering and snapping. Of course, aluminum poles add to the tent's price, but the added expense is well worth it in the long run.

Cleaning Tent Poles

It is a good idea to keep your pole joints clean and grit-free. If you hear or feel some scratching when you are fitting the poles together, simply dunk the joints into water and dry them thoroughly.

Repairing a Broken Pole

If you do not have the right tools, a broken pole can be a tragedy that renders your otherwise hardy shelter into a droopy, flapping mess of nylon. Good thing the remedy is featherweight and foolproof: a small aluminum repair sleeve that probably comes standard with the purchase of your tent.

Simply slide the tube over the broken section and duct tape it securely into place (fig. 5-2). Take care when sliding this section into and out of the pole sleeve, because it will tend to snag on the fabric.

Fig. 5-2. Tent-pole Repair Sleeve

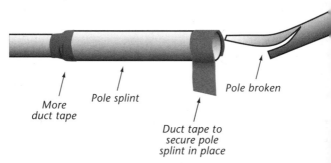

More
duct tape

Pole splint

Duct tape to
secure pole
splint in place

Pole broken

Back at home, contact the tent manufacturer about fixing or replacing the injured pole; most are covered under an unlimited warranty.

Repairing a Pole Burr

Burrs or snags typically happen near pole joints (fig. 5-3)—the result of recklessly snapping the sections together rather than fitting each section into place one by one (see An Ounce of Prevention: Do Not Snap!). Inspect your pole joints on a regular basis and keep them smooth. Finally—a use for that file on your pocket tool! Other smoothing devices: a piece of sandpaper, an emery board, or even a flat rock, if you are desperate.

Fig. 5-3. Tent-pole Burr

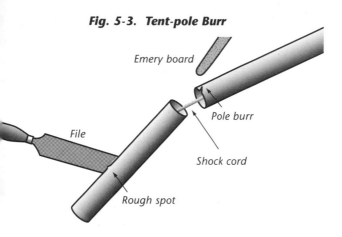

Emery board

Pole burr

File

Shock cord

Rough spot

Replacing Broken or Stretched-out Shock Cord

If you routinely camp in really cold weather or if the shock cord in your tent poles isn't up to snuff, you may someday find that there just isn't enough snap left in the cord to secure all your pole sections together easily. It can be done with a large dose of patience, but who has that when darkness is falling and the wind is kicking up?

If this happens to you, the easiest thing to do is to send the pole(s) to a pro (see the appendix, Repair Facility Reference Guide, at the back of this book) who can rethread them with fresh cord. This operation can be performed at home, but it is rarely worth the headache, and you run the risk of damaging the pole parts even more.

An Ounce of Prevention: Do Not Snap!

It is tempting to just yank your tent poles apart and let the shock cord snap the sections together, but this is one of the most common ways that poles are damaged. The impact on the pole tips results in cracks and splits. Instead, gently separate the sections and fold them together, starting in the center of each pole rather than at an end (this minimizes stress on the shock cord).

WATER PROBLEMS

The bad news: Leaks happen. You *will*, at some point in your camping life, experience some wetness in your tent. Leaks happen for one of the following reasons:

- ✔ seams are improperly sealed or not sealed at all
- ✔ floor material is faulty or worn
- ✔ rain fly's waterproofing has worn off
- ✔ condensation occurs

The good news: You can prevent or minimize condensation (see earlier in this chapter), and you can fix all the other causes. After you determine why the tent is leaking (it is not always obvious), chances are that the solution is simple and not at all costly.

Sealing Seams

These days, most good tents come with factory seam-taped rain flies and floors. When shopping for a tent, look for this key feature, which adds a few bucks to the price tag but is well worth the money. If your tent did not come sealed or if you just want added protection, buy a good seam sealer and get to work.

Pick a warm, sunny day and set up your tent in the yard with the rain fly inside out. (Always seal the uncoated inside seams of the fly and tent floor.) Stake the tent and fly out tautly so the seams are stretched and ready to drink up that sealer. Make sure the seams are clean, then wipe them with a bit of alcohol on a cotton ball to make them more receptive to the sealer.

Paint each and every seam on the fly and around the inside of the tent floor with sealer. For tough-to-reach corners and places where webbing attaches to fabric, apply some sealer with a syringe, injecting it into place.

Be patient and let the sealer dry thoroughly before you pack up the tent and fly, or else the fabric will bond to itself—an ugly and unfortunate mess.

Reviving a Tent Fly's Waterproofing

Has this happened to you? Your rain fly, which used to make water bead up and roll right off, now gets saturated and saggy. The fly seems to be in good repair otherwise. One possible solution is to reapply waterproofing, or DWR, to the fly.

Set the tent up in your yard on a sunny day and start by giving it a good cleaning (see Cleaning and Storing Your Tent). Then apply a spray-on DWR treatment (ask at your outdoor shop for one specifically designed for tents) as evenly as you can to the exterior of the fly and let it dry completely before repacking. (See chapter 1, Fabrics, for additional information on spray-on waterproofing.)

If the waterproof coating on the inside of your rain fly starts to peel or flake, you can rejuvenate it the same as the tent floor (see the next section).

Reviving a Tent Floor's Waterproofing

You fall asleep to the pleasant, hypnotic sound of rain drumming on your tent. About four hours later, you wake up because your feet are cold and clammy. No wonder—there is a puddle of water at the bottom of the tent, and your down sleeping bag is a sodden sponge!

Tent floors are subjected to rocks, roots, sticks, and pricks, among other hardships, so it should come as no surprise if your tent floor eventually gives way to a bit of dampness. Especially if the tent is old or inexpensive, it may need a fresh coat of waterproofing to jump-start it back to life. If the floor coating is flaking, peeling, or just plain tired, here is what to do.

First, clean the tent and remove any residual coating by putting the tent in your washing machine. That's right—this is the *one* time when you are allowed to go this route. As described above in Cleaning and Storing Your Tent, the washer and dryer wreak havoc on the waterproof coatings of your tent. But because you need to strip the old coatings in order to replace them, the washing machine is your best bet. Run it through the gentle cycle with cold water and a touch of mild powdered soap (such as Ivory Flakes). Then pop it in the dryer on low heat for about 5 minutes. Remove the tent and hang it until completely dry. Then scrub the tent floor with a vegetable brush to remove any remaining flakes of waterproof coating.

When the tent is clean and dry, set it up and flip it onto its side. Using a polyurethane product that is designed specifically or the task (check your outdoor shop for the best options), simply follow the instructions and evenly paint the outside of the floor. Let it dry completely before packing it away. **Note:** The new coating may make the consistency of the fabric a bit waxier and crinklier, but performance will only be improved.

Fig. 5-4. Making a Ground Cloth

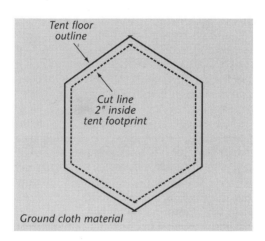

Tent floor outline

Cut line 2" inside tent footprint

Ground cloth material

A Groundsheet Is a Tent's Best Friend

The best thing you can do to prolong the life of your tent and prevent any floor leakage is to use a groundsheet. Sure, it takes up precious space in your pack, but if the trip promises to be wet or if you are protective of your new investment, the decision is a no-brainer. Many tent makers now offer custom-made groundsheets for a tent of any shape, but these can cost around

$100 and weigh much more than a homemade one. Making your own groundsheet will take only a few minutes and cost you less than a fast-food meal.

You will need a large sheet of waterproof material. There are loads of options: an old vinyl shower curtain, a piece of polyethylene from the hardware store, nylon from a fabric store, even a piece of Tyvek housewrap scavenged from a construction site. (Tyvek is extremely lightweight, but it is not the most durable choice. In fact, it will probably last only a single season.) You will also need scissors, a marker, some duct tape (of course!), and grommets (optional).

1. Lay the uncut groundsheet out and set up your tent on top of it (without its rain fly and vestibule, if it has one). Stake the tent out tautly.

2. Using the marker, trace the outline of the tent onto the ground sheet.

3. Trim the excess from the groundsheet, following an invisible line two inches *inside* the line you traced around the tent (fig. 5-4). This is to prevent any overhanging fabric, which would direct rain underneath your tent floor. This is very important! When trimming is complete, no portion of the groundsheet should extend beyond the footprint of the tent.

    If you use nylon (a good choice because of its light weight and durability), cut *exactly* along the traced line. Then sew a 2-inch hem around the perimeter of the groundsheet to prevent the fabric from fraying.

4. (optional) If you plan on using grommets, instead of cutting uniformly two inches inside your tracing, cut the corners right *on* the line and arc the sides inward two inches. Then attach grommets to the corners. Now you can firmly attach the groundsheet by looping the grommets over the tent-pole tips when you set up the

tent. Plus, you can use the groundsheet as a pack cover in the rain or rig it as a tarp for a cooking shelter or vestibule extender.

Duct Tape Tip

If you opt to use a shower curtain, polyethylene, or Tyvek for a groundsheet, cut long strips of duct tape in half lengthwise. Then carefully fold the strips over the edges of the groundsheet. This will protect the edges from tearing or shredding.

CHAPTER 6.

Sleeping Bags and Pads

IMAGINE THIS:
You have spent a day's pay on a cushy, self-inflating sleeping pad and you are ready to reap the benefits. But after a close encounter with a jagged branch, the mattress of your dreams is fatally wounded with an inch-long gash. Do you have the surgical skills to bring it back to life? Or will you sleep on the cold, hard ground?

Maybe you marched too many miles, labored up too many hills, carried too heavy a load, or dodged too many raindrops. Whatever the reason, sometimes you just need to crawl into a fluffy, cozy cocoon at the end of the day. When the going gets tough, a good sleeping bag and sleeping pad are like a sanctuary.

If you are looking for a great warmth-to-weight ratio, a down sleeping bag is the way to go. Fluffy down plumules also last longer than any synthetic fiber. Synthetic bags are best for people on a budget or those who often find themselves camping in wet conditions.

Quality Counts

When shopping for a bag, crawl inside to check its size. You want plenty of space to squirm, but not too much, because your body has to heat that space. If you camp in cold weather, be sure to have about six inches of extra room at the feet to store your camera, water bottles, and other gear you want to keep dry.

The key to a sleeping bag's success is "loft," a term that refers to the bag's thickness and its ability to capture and hold the heat of your body. You are your bag's primary caregiver, and your number-one goal is maintaining this loft. Over the years, a bag will inevitably deflate a bit, but with proper care, a high-quality sleeping bag should last as long as you.

CARING FOR AND STORING DOWN BAGS

The main drawback with down is that if you get it wet, it degenerates into a clumpy mess. Make every effort to keep a down bag from getting wet. If your down filling does get wet and clump up, declump it by gently working the clusters apart. Dry the bag and check for more clumps.

Over time, down can shift around inside the bag's baffles (mesh barriers inside your bag that hold the insulation in place), so you will want to redistribute it. With the bag flat on the ground, simply push the pillowy stuff around inside the bag until it is uniformly distributed.

Never, never, never store your down sleeping bag in its itty-bitty stuff sack for long-term storage! The longer your bag stays compressed, the more fluffiness it will lose. It is fine to use a stuff sack while you are on the trail, but the minute you get home, release it from that confined space, give it a good fluff, and store it in a place where the loft can stay lofty. You can spread it out under your bed, hang it in a closet, or place it in a big, breathable storage bag with a drawstring top. If you do not have a storage sack, use a king-size pillowcase. Store your bag in a cool, dark, and very dry place, such as a basement (if yours is historically dry) or closet.

CARING FOR SYNTHETIC BAGS

Synthetic sleeping bags still provide some insulation when they get damp or wet, whereas down fails miserably. Although it is not exactly blissful to sleep in a wet synthetic bag, it is certainly more pleasant than passing the night in a wet down one.

Synthetic bags' number-one enemy is heat. When drying a synthetic bag in a clothes dryer, be sure to use the lowest possible dryer setting and monitor the drying process.

CLEANING SLEEPING BAGS

Wash a sleeping bag only when necessary. Unlike your long johns, your sleeping bag does not need to be washed after every trip. You do need to keep the sleeping-bag lining clean, however. Here is what happens: your average grungy outdoorsperson climbs into the sleeping bag with few or no clothes on. Soon the bag's lining is contaminated with bug repellent, sunscreen, trail dust, and body oil. Eventually all that can make its way into the insulation, and loft begins to die a slow death. The moral: Do not sleep naked.

Wash your bag maybe once a year, unless something really sloppy happens such as a spilled pot of soup or fuel bottle leak. Before washing, make sure all the zippers and Velcro tabs are closed. If they are left open, they can abrade delicate linings and coatings.

When you do wash your bag, make a trip to the Laundromat, so you can use jumbo, front-loading washers without an agitator in the center. The agitator in most home washing machines can twist and damage a sleeping bag's insulation fibers and baffle material. Use cold water, the gentle cycle, and a mild, nondetergent soap (found at specialty outdoor shops or natural food stores). Then wash the bag a second time without the soap to remove any lingering suds.

When transferring your bag to a clothes dryer, be careful not to drag or stretch it—you can easily damage the interior baffles. Go for the largest dryer you can find and set it on a cool to medium setting. Check the bag periodically to make sure the fabric is not scorching hot and the insulation is not bunching. It may take close to two hours to thoroughly dry a bag, so be patient. Contrary to some popular advice, *do not* put a tennis ball or sneaker in the dryer with your bag—this will only damage the insulation. You can, however, place clean, dry bath towels in the dryer to suck up some of the moisture. Check the towels periodically and swap wet ones for dry ones.

Or, if it is a warm, sunny day, you can hang your bag lengthwise from a clothesline or lay it flat on a picnic table.

Never dry clean your sleeping bag. The chemicals wreak havoc on the materials.

An Ounce of Prevention: Liners

To keep your sleeping bag clean and avoid having to wash it, use a sleeping bag liner made of silk, cotton (in summertime), or a synthetic material. Not only do liners keep your bag clean, they are wonderfully comfortable—like slipping in between clean sheets. Unlike a sleeping bag, a liner can be washed after every trip.

REPAIRING SLEEPING BAGS

Most field repairs to a sleeping bag involve fabric (see chapter 1) or zippers (see chapter 2). To prevent your bag from getting soggy and losing loft, let your bag air out on a sunny rock or branch as you break camp. Pack it up last. This gives your accumulated body moisture a chance to evaporate.

SELF-INFLATING SLEEPING PADS

If you have never slept on a self-inflating mattress, beware. Once you try one, you will never go back to the old-fashioned closed-cell foam type (unless you decide to use both). The only reason *not* to carry a self-inflater is if you are really trying to pinch some pounds from your load—self-inflaters are significantly heavier than closed-cell foam pads.

The gist of a self-inflater is this: it is a simple slab of open-celled foam encased in a nylon sheath. When the valve at one corner is opened, air enters the chamber and puffs the foam up to full capacity (anywhere between $3/4$ inch for the ultralight pads to $2^1/_2$ inches for the supercushy ones). Then you just close the valve and you have a portable mattress. After your snooze, just open the valve again, roll the mattress tight to squeeze out the air, close the valve, and it is a compact bundle ready to pack.

An Ounce of Prevention: Save Your Breath

You know why they call them "self-inflaters"? Because they require little to no help from you when it comes to puffing up. It can be tempting to blow into the valve to get your bed made promptly, but your pad will fare better if you just open the valve, lay the pad out flat, and let it do its own thing. Your breath contains lots of water, which can build up inside the foam to cause mildew.

CLOSED-CELL FOAM PADS

Closed-cell foam pads used to be smooth-surfaced, but now there are all kinds of ridged designs to provide more comfort. These pads are light and incredibly durable, but they need to be kept away from direct sources of heat so they do not melt. If a closed-cell foam pad gets a tear in it, a little duct tape will mend it. You can cut away damaged portions and use the scraps for other insulating purposes. Here is one idea.

Make a backpacking bed for Fido. Cut a pooch-sized square of foam to pack along so your dog does not nudge you off your pad in the middle of the night.

Duct Tape Tip

Use duct tape and a scrap of closed-cell foam pad to make a water-bottle cozy. Cut a square of foam sized to wrap perfectly around your water bottle, then duct-tape it in place. Slip a bottle of hot soup or cocoa into the cozy after breakfast, and at lunchtime you will be treated to a warm drink.

CLEANING AND STORING SLEEPING PADS

Like all your precious gear, pads should always be stored clean and dry. When a pad gets grimy, just wipe it down with warm, soapy water, then rinse and air dry. If the valve on a self-inflating pad gets gunked up with grit, blast it with a garden hose, then be sure to let the pad dry thoroughly with the valve open.

All pads should be stored flat; self-inflaters should go to rest with the valves open. This is because foam has surprisingly good memory and might hesitate to puff up if it is rolled into a tight wad for too long.

REPAIRING A LEAK IN A SELF-INFLATING PAD

If your self-inflating pad springs a leak in the field, you had better be ready with the right repair tools, because a gashed self-inflating pad is almost as bad as no pad at all.

Sometimes it is painfully obvious where the leak is; other times you have to be Sherlock Holmes. If you cannot pinpoint the hole by listening for the telltale hiss, submerge the pad in water (either the tub back home or a still pool in the field) and look for air bubbles.

Fig. 6-1. Fixing a Leak in a Self-inflating Pad

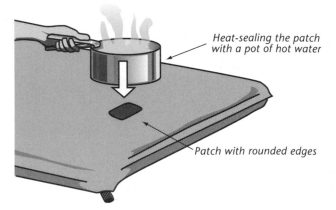

Heat-sealing the patch with a pot of hot water

Patch with rounded edges

Once you have located the leak, fixing it is a snap with a few essential tools if you follow these steps.
1. Put a pot of water on your backpacking stove to boil.
2. Clean the problem area with an alcohol cleaning pad from your first-aid kit. Open the valve.
3. Cut the patch. Most self-inflaters come with swatches of the proper material. If you do not have the repair kit that came with the pad, use whatever nylon patch you have on hand. Make sure the patch is about $1/2$ inch larger in diameter than the hole, and do not forget to round the edges so they are less prone to peeling.
4. Smear a generous gob of Seam Grip into the gash. If it is a small puncture hole, inject the Seam Grip into place using an irrigation syringe.

5. Apply more Seam Grip to the area surrounding the wound—about $1/2$ inch around the circumference of the gash should do it.
6. Place the patch atop the adhesive, then set the pot of boiled water on top of that (fig. 6-1). The heat from the pot acts as a quick sealer. After a few seconds, lift the pot to make sure no adhesive has oozed out from under the patch. If it has, wipe it off and replace the pot.
7. Let the pot sit on your pad until the water is cool, about half an hour.

CHAPTER 7.

Stoves

> **IMAGINE THIS:**
> *All day long you have been toiling up Mount Whatsitsname, dreaming about a hot cup of cocoa and a delicious bowl of minestrone soup. When you finally make it to camp, you commence dinner-making, only to find that your stove has a case of the flu—it sputters and coughs and emits only a luke-warm yellow flame. This could be catastrophic! Will you be dining on cold cacciatore for the next few days? Or can you coax your stove back to life and eat like royalty?*

Choosing a backpacking stove can be a bewildering affair. At the store you will undoubtedly be faced with shelves of complex-looking contraptions with metal wires, tubes, valves, and thingamajigs, plus an array of fuel choices that range from variously sized and shaped prefilled metal canisters to fill-it-yourself bottles and one-gallon cans of fuel. There are a number of factors to consider in your stove buying decision: the terrain and conditions you frequent, your tolerance for fiddling and cleaning, and the types of meals you choose to cook. That said, most good backpacking stoves can be categorized according to fuel type and they fall into two basic categories: canister-style stoves and liquid fuel burners.

Canister stoves are available in various shapes and sizes, but all contain some blend of pressurized fuels that are released under pressure as a burnable gas. Canister stoves tend to be cheap, simple, quiet, and convenient. On the downside, their elaborately packaged fuel is more expensive, older canisters can be difficult to recycle, and they are finicky in truly cold weather. Stoves that run on pressurized canisters will still work down to about freezing, but they require some extra care.

The majority of liquid fuel stoves have remote, refillable fuel bottles. (**Note:** There are a few exceptions—stoves that burn liquid fuel stored in small, integral tanks below the burner.) Although not as convenient as canister stoves (they require a pumping mechanism to pressurize the tank and deliver fuel to the burner), liquid fuel stoves are best for colder weather and extended trips.

Most liquid fuel stoves burn white gas, most often found in gallon containers under the Coleman name. White gas is the fuel of choice because it packs more BTUs for its weight than other liquid fuel, including automotive gasoline or kerosene. Some stoves, called multifuel stoves, burn a variety of fuels, which is a boon if you are traveling someplace where white gas is unavailable. If given the option, though, always choose white gas, because it burns cleaner and hotter and you will end up spending less time cleaning your stove. As a rule, stoves that run on white gas perform better in cold weather.

Quality Counts

It is tempting, but do not use the dregs of that old gallon of white gas that has been sitting in your garage for a couple years. Splurge (five bucks) and buy a fresh can of the stuff each season. It will spare your poor old stove a lot of trouble—clogging, sputtering, and general grumpiness. Always use fresh fuel for the best performance.

An Ounce of Prevention: Packing Stove and Fuel

Stoves and fuel require a bit of packing precision—you do not want a bent pot support or a leaky fuel bottle to come between you and a hot meal. Some stoves come with nifty padded cases; another good way to ensure protection for your stove is to pack it inside your nesting cookware. Stash fuel bottles in an outside pocket of your pack if possible. If not, double-bag the bottles in hardy zipper-lock bags, then pack them near the bottom of your pack so that if a leak does happen, it will not contaminate all your food and gear.

USING CANISTER STOVES

Once a canister stove goes kaput, there is not much you can do to fix it. However, there are a few things you can do to boost the performance of your canister stove and keep it cooking longer.

Bringing full fuel canisters.

As you burn fuel, the pressure in the canister decreases, and with it, efficiency. So start each trip with full canisters and save those half-spent ones for warm-weather trips.

Warming the canisters.

As the canisters burn fuel, they get colder and more sluggish. To solve this, you can do a couple of things. First, you can tape one of those disposable or reusable hand warmers to the bottom of the canister. This helps enormously. Or you can set the canister in about one inch of water. Warm water works best, but cool water will help as well.

Duct Tape Tip

If your stove runs on prefilled, pressurized canisters, make a custom-sized canister cozy to boost performance in cold weather. From a scrap of closed-cell foam pad, cut a square sized to fit around your canister, then duct-tape it in place. It should not fit so tightly that it cannot be slipped off easily when it's time to change canisters.

Setting up a wind block.

This is a bit different from wrapping a complete windscreen around the burner as you would do with a liquid fuel stove (see below). With a canister stove, in which the fuel tank is attached directly to the burner, a full windscreen can actually generate too much heat, resulting in melted control dials. To create an effective wind block, simply nestle your stove behind a rock or tree, or use pot lids or other items you have on hand. Just be sure there is plenty of ventilation around the burner.

An Ounce of Prevention: Do Not Forget Matches

No matter what type of stove you use, remember to have a couple different lighting tools on hand. Lighters work great until your fingers are cold and numb, so play it safe and always pack a box of waterproof matches as a backup.

USING LIQUID FUEL STOVES

These are more field repairable than canister stoves, which is a big plus. The most important tip for maintaining your stove is to read its instruction manual and pack it along with you. Because the mechanics of stoves differ according to brand, much of what you need to know is specific to your model. These manuals provide detailed instructions on how to troubleshoot your particular stove. Entrust the little manual to its own zipper-lock baggie and stow it safely away in your stove storage sack. In a nutshell, that little booklet will save you if you end up having trouble in the field. That said, however, here are a few concepts and tips that are general enough to apply to most liquid fuel stoves.

An Ounce of Prevention: Caring for Your Stove

Before every trip, give your stove a tune-up. This means disassembling it as much as possible, wiping down all the parts (fig. 7-1), greasing all the O-rings with a silicone lubrication, and checking that you have a well-stocked repair kit to bring into the field with you. Closely inspect all your O-rings to make sure they are in good shape. The rubber should be soft and supple. If not, lubricate the rings with a silicone lubrication. And always be sure to have the appropriate spares in your repair kit.

Priming

It is imperative to know how to properly prime—preheat—your stove. Many people complain that priming is a royal pain largely based on luck, but this just is not the case. Priming may

Fig. 7-1. Stove

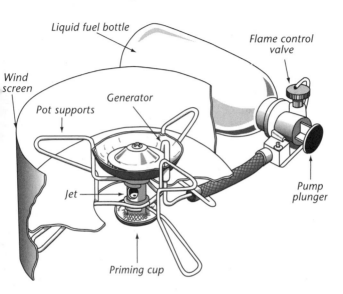

be somewhat of an art, but it is easy to master with a little practice. Just do the practicing at home, not in the field.

Generally, priming entails filling a fuel cup on the bottom of the stove with gas, lighting the fuel, and letting it burn down while the stove heats up. When the gas is mostly burned off and the flame is similar to that of a candle, it is time to start the stove. Turn the flame control on, but keep it at a low blue flame for a couple of minutes before cranking it up. If the flame dies out before you are able to ignite it, quickly turn the control knob a bit and try to relight. Hopefully, the stove will still be warm enough that your stove will burst to life. If not, or if you are faced with a giant yellow flare-up, let the stove cool down and start all over again. Remember, practice makes perfect.

Cold-weather Tip

When the weather turns cold, camp stoves inevitably get balky, but you can boost your stove's efficiency and make that hot drink happen a wee bit faster if you use a windscreen. This will drastically improve boil times. If your stove did not come with a windscreen, make one out of a couple layers of heavy-duty tin foil or a piece of roof flashing from a home improvement store.

Duct Tape Tip

For a more stable stove, cut a square of old closed-cell foam pad sized to fit the base of your backpacking stove. Wrap the foam generously with duct tape for insulation, and you have a stable cooking platform that works great in the snow.

Cleaning the Jet

The jet is a tiny hole inside your stove that transforms the liquid fuel into a burnable fine mist. With normal use, this jet becomes clogged with carbon, resulting in a sputtering yellow flame rather than the desired hot, steady, blue one.

Many stoves these days are equipped with an integral jet cleaner, so all you have to do is turn the stove upside down and a small needle cleans out the hole automatically. (If you are in the market for a new stove, look for this feature—it makes life a lot easier.)

If there is not an automatic jet-cleaning feature on your stove, disassemble the generator according to the instruction manual and prick the hole open with a cleaning tool.

Servicing O-rings

Those little black circular gaskets that appear at various places on your stove and fuel bottle are critical to good performance. If they are cracked, dried out, or otherwise hurting, fuel is apt to start leaking, which is wasteful, causes performance to suffer, and, most importantly, is downright dangerous. If your O-rings' rubber is not soft and supple, lubricate them with something slimy such as saliva, olive oil, or lip balm. Or replace them with the appropriate spares from your repair kit.

Lubricating the Pump Seal

On stoves with detached fuel bottles, the pump assembly is inserted inside the fuel bottle. On stoves with an integral fuel tank, the pump assembly is built into the fuel tank.

You will know your pump needs some TLC if there is no resistance to speak of when you pump. In this case, unscrew the pump assembly and take a look at the leather pump cup. This little circle of leather needs to remain supple and moist in order to create the desired pressure inside the fuel bottle. If the pump cup is dry, brittle, or cracked, apply some lubrication: olive oil, saliva, or lip balm.

CHAPTER 8.

Water Filters

IMAGINE THIS:
You have just marched uphill for four hours and both your water bottles are bone dry. You stop for the night at a lovely lake, whip out your trusty water filter, and commence making potable water. After you have pumped just a few ounces, your filter stages a mutiny. Pumping becomes excruciatingly difficult. Do you stick your head in the lake and start slurping out of desperation, or can you coax your filter back to working order?

There are a number of ways to make water safe to drink. You can boil it, but sometimes boiling is not very practical for backpackers because it requires that you carry lots of extra fuel and it takes quite a lot of time to boil and cool your drinking water. However, boiling water safely removes all pathogens.

Using iodine or chlorine tablets is another option, often favored by seasoned outdoorsfolks because it is weight- and cost-effective. A bottle of iodine costs less than ten dollars, lasts for many trips, and weighs only a few ounces. The main drawbacks with iodine or chlorine are the swimming poolish taste (which can be remedied with a sugary drink mix) and the fact that iodine and chlorine cannot kill tenacious hard-shelled protozoans like *Cryptosporidium*. Also, pregnant women and people with compromised immune systems should not use iodine.

Using a water filter is quick, easy, and in most cases quite safe (some cannot remove all viruses), which is why so many backpackers carry them. Water filters are portable devices that separate the cooties from the water with a few strokes of a pump. Filters do have a serious drawback, though: they tend to clog, which can be a royal pain when you are thirsty.

Make sure you buy the right filter. If you will be camping with your family of five, opt for a bigger, heavier unit designed to handle lots of water. If it is just you and the Appalachian Trail, save the ounces and go with a smaller, more packable filter. Make sure the filter is designed for your intended use.

Read the label. Be sure it filters out *Giardia lamblia* at a minimum. If you are concerned about viruses, look for a filter that claims to remove them as well.

The best stores have filters on display that you can fondle, pump, and prod. Play with them. This will give you an idea of how ergonomic a filter is.

Ask lots of questions. Talk to salespeople who have used different filters. Inquire about field maintainability, longevity of filter elements, and general word of mouth.

Quality Counts

If your filter of choice does not come with a prefilter, fork over the extra bucks to get it. Sometimes sold separately, these devices fit on the end of the intake hose to remove the larger chunks of sediment that can clog your filter. This will save you loads of headaches in the field and also extend the life of your filter element.

CLEANING AND STORING A WATER FILTER

The key to successful filtering is to keep the filter element clean. Be good to your filter and you will triple or quadruple its life, not to mention help it filter more efficiently. Filters come with elaborate cleaning/maintenance instructions, which you should follow exactly and carry with you in a zipper-lock bag. Preventive cleaning before and after each trip—especially before long-term storage—is a wise course of action.

Give it a bleach job. At the beginning and end of the hiking season (at least), pump a solution of one capful of household bleach and one quart of tap water through the filter.

Store it properly. Avoid storing your filter in a zipper-lock baggie or any other type of nonbreathable sack. Instead, opt for a mesh bag that promotes airflow and ample drying time.

If the pumping becomes difficult, break open the filter's instructions and get to work. Cleaning techniques vary from brand to brand, but some general tips will work for most models.

Backwash it. When output starts to slow, detach the intake hose and attach it to the filter outlet. Then pump away to send a backwash of clean water through the filter, loosening some of the accumulated gunk. After backwashing or before storage, pump a diluted bleach solution through the filter to sanitize it. **Note:** Not all filters can be backwashed. Check your manual to see if yours can.

Scrub the ceramic element. If your filter is ceramic, you can drastically improve output by removing the cylinder and scrubbing it with a toothbrush (an old one specifically designated for filter cleaning, not the one you use on your teeth!). After scrubbing, swish the filter around in the water and it is good to go.

USING YOUR FILTER

Your filter is an important device that could mean the difference between being really sick for a couple of days or not. Follow these tips on how to use your filter with care so it can take care of you.

Handle it carefully. Dropping a filter can cause tiny cracks that let bugs through.

Keep it cozy. In cold weather, do not let residual water in your filter freeze up. This can also cause the filter element to crack. Be sure to rid the filter of all water when you are done using it. And on really cold nights, wrap it in a towel or tee shirt and stow it in your sleeping bag.

Do not be a slave driver. Use your filter only when you need it. For instance, there is no need to filter water that you will boil for spaghetti or hot cocoa.

Use a prefilter. If you need to fashion one on your own, wrap a paper coffee filter or a piece of cotton cloth around the intake hose and secure it with a rubber band.

Start with the cleanest water you can. Do not make your filter work harder than need be. Seek out pools rather than currents, because moving water stirs up sand and debris. Keep the intake hose off the bottom of the lake or riverbed, where it tends to suck up sand, mud, muck, leaf detritus, and who knows what else.

Let water settle. Dip up a pot full and set it aside to let the suspended solids settle out. An hour or two helps, but leave water overnight if possible. This simple step gives you cleaner water to process, which can triple the time between filter cleanings or filter replacement.

An Ounce of Prevention: Choose Your Water Wisely

If given the choice of filtering your drinking water from a roiling, brown, silty river or a still, clear pool, you will go with the latter, right? Of course. A couple other tips: Poke around and make sure there are no obvious signs of animal activity. In other words, if there is a huge pile of bear poop on the riverbank, head upstream. Of course, there is no guarantee that there is not another bear poop right around the bend, but minimize your exposure to cooties wherever you can. Pumping at or near the water's source is always a good idea.

Table 8-1.
Troubleshooting Guide to Water Filters

What Happens	Why It Happens
No water enters the intake hose when you pump.	Filter needs to be "primed."
Filter is extremely difficult to pump.	The filter is clogged.
Water leaks from the plastic filter housing.	Usually an O-ring or seal problem.

Duct Tape Tip

If the intake or output hose springs a leak (a crack or a puncture), wrap it neatly with a few turns of duct tape. Or, if the wound happens near either end of a hose, just detach the hose, snip away the damaged section with scissors or a sharp blade, and reattach the hose to the filter.

How to Fix It	How to Prevent It
Varies by brand. Read owner's manual. Do not worry; it is usually a very simple, easy manuever.	All seals need to be airtight so filter is like a vaccuum, sucking up water. Keep the filter free of grit; one tiny grain of Colorado River silt can disrupt a seal.
Clean the filter as per the owner's manual (varies by brand).	There is no way to avoid having to clean your filter altogether, but you can extract maximum efficiency from it by letting water settle before pumping and then using a prefilter.
Dissasemble the filter and inspect all seals. Lubricate with silicone or replace as needed.	Keep those O-rings supple with silicone lubrication.

CHAPTER 9.

Cookware

> ***IMAGINE THIS:***
> *You have finally reached camp and commenced the dinner-making process. You have a decadent feast planned for your friends—home-dried bolognese sauce over fettuccine, and fudge brownies for dessert. When you unpack the cookware, you discover rusty gouges covering the bottom of the trusty nonstick pot that cost you a fortune. Cooking in it will not kill you, but could you have taken better care of your cookware to preserve that all-important nonstick coating? You bet your biscuits!*

Cooking pots come in all sorts of shapes, sizes, and materials. To decide what is right for you, consider the types of camp meals you cook, how many you cook for, your threshold for the weight you carry, your durability needs—and, of course, your budget.

Aluminum pots are the most economical, which might explain why boy scouts have been relying on them for decades to cook their franks and beans. Aluminum is also quite lightweight, which makes it a good option for backpackers. But, alas, aluminum dents easily, and unless it is coated with a nonstick finish (which boosts the price), it requires some serious elbow grease to clean.

Stainless-steel pots are a bit heavier than aluminum, but they can stand up to years of backcountry abuse. Stainless also has a slicker, easier-to-clean coating, so your macaroni and cheese–tuna surprise will not become one of your pot's permanent features.

Titanium pots pack a hefty price tag, but if you are a true ounce-counter, you may be seduced by their light weight. Titanium is surprisingly strong, but food likes to stick to it, although not quite as much as to uncoated aluminum.

Composite pots are usually built from a thin layer of aluminum on the outside (to trim ounces) and a layer of stainless steel on the inside (to prevent sticking). It is a happy medium, but this type is not as widely available as the others.

Once you have decided on the type of metal that is right for you, consider these features:

- ✔ **Tight-fitting lids keep heat inside where you want it.**
- ✔ **Black outer finishes absorb heat faster and boost cooking efficiency.**
- ✔ **Rounded bottom edges are easier to clean, plus they help heat creep up the pot sides for even distribution.**
- ✔ **The best way to go is with pot grippers used with plain, handleless pots. Swing or bail handles are usually flimsy and they can heat up quickly, which results in burnt fingers.**

CARING FOR YOUR POTS

Nonstick pots bear a pretty hefty price tag, so treat them with respect. Metal can scratch the coating off the bottom of your pot, resulting in rust spots, so opt for plastic or wooden cutlery (not metal) for stirring your soup.

Quality Counts

When shopping for kitchen accessories, go for the stuff labeled "Lexan." It is a sturdy, lightweight, and heat-resistant plastic that is ideally suited for camping. For bowls, plates, and cutlery, Lexan is the way to go. You will also find Lexan cups, but most veteran backpackers prefer insulated, lidded plastic cups (coffee travel mugs) because they keep drinks hotter longer.

Pack your cookware carefully. That means packing them in the inner, padded sanctum of your pack, not near the bottom where they might get crushed or dented each time you drop your pack.

Duct Tape Tip

Want a handy place to store a stash of duct tape? Wrap a healthy length around the handle of your largest utensil (a wooden spoon if you carry one, or even your Lexan fork or eating spoon). When you need some tape, just unravel the proper amount, rip it off, and start repairing! A mini duct-tape dispenser!

CARING FOR YOUR POCKETKNIFE

Learn to take care of your trusty pocketknife, that wonderful tool that chops your food, spreads your peanut butter, whittles your fire-starting twigs, helps with gear repairs, and opens the cold bottles of beer at trip's end.

When your pocket tool is clean, make sure all the hinges and joints are in good working order by opening and closing them a number of times. If the joints are grabby, apply a drop of cooking oil to the hinges.

Sharpening Your Pocket Knife

A dull blade is more than a nuisance, it is downright dangerous. Dull blades tend to skid around the cutting surface, often resulting in cuts where you do not want them (like your hand) rather than where you do (like your onion). Knife sharpening is an art. There are a variety of techniques, but here is the simplest way to stay on the cutting edge:

Fig. 9-1. Knife Sharpening

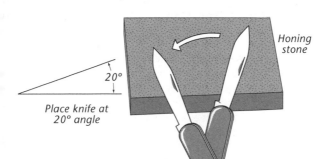

1. Lubricate a honing stone with water.
2. With the blade positioned at about a 20-degree angle to the stone (fig. 9-1), draw the blade toward you by flicking your wrist. Changing the angle of the blade creates different effects.
3. Flip the knife over and sharpen the other side of the blade, this time working away from your body. Be sure to make the same number of strokes on each side. Do ten strokes on one side, then ten on the other, then repeat. The key is to apply steady, even pressure on the stone. Do not push too hard.
4. Test the knife by lightly scraping the blade across your thumbnail. If you have removed a thin layer of nail, your knife is good to go.

CLEANING YOUR COOKWARE AND DISHES

If your pots do not have a nonstick coating, you can be much more nonchalant about cleaning them. Pack a steel wool scouring pad if you want. But nonstick pots, which are increasingly popular, require a bit more TLC, just like those fancy ones in your kitchen at home. Do not use anything abrasive to clean them—no steel wool pads, just elbow grease and a soft sponge.

Lost your scrubby sponge? Use sand, a pinecone, or ashes from the campfire—they make terrific abrasive agents. Just toss a handful into the wash pot and scrub with your hand or a cloth. Snow also works great in wintertime. **Note:** These natural abrasives are safe to use with nonstick pots; just don't overdo it. If you can get away with just a "soft" cleaning, do it.

If you are in charge of dish duty for the night, fill up the biggest pot with water, add a squirt of biodegradable soap if the grease factor is high, heat it up on the stove, then go to it. If there are hard-to-scrub remnants caked on, bring the water to a boil and let it cool till your hands can stand the heat. Warm, soapy water on a chilly night makes dish duty much more bearable. Plus, you walk away with the cleanest hands in camp, which is quite a luxury.

On short trips, leave the soap behind. But on trips of a week or more, grease will build up on your pots and utensils, so pack a small bottle of unscented, biodegradable camp soap.

Never wash dishes directly in a water source. Human food remnants and soap do not belong in a backcountry lake or river. Move at least 200 feet away from the water. If there are lots of chunks of food left over in the wash pot, filter them out with a bandanna and add them to your trash bag. This is a much better option than dumping remnants on the ground, where critters can find them and, in turn, become conditioned to pester campers for snacks.

When you are doing dishes for a large crew, a lightweight collapsible bucket is great. (This type of bucket also does double duty as a group water hauler, for bringing water up from a river or lake.) Fill the bucket with clean rinse water for that final dip.

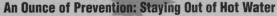

An Ounce of Prevention: Staying Out of Hot Water

Need a foolproof dish-duty avoidance tactic? Just confess your hatred of doing dishes, then make good by doing other chores, such as helping with the food preparation, pumping water, or hanging the food bags. There is usually someone in the group who hates doing those things as much as you hate dishes, and who will gladly trade chores.

CLEANING YOUR POCKETKNIFE

Boil some water and let it cool for about 5 minutes. Then drop in your knife—with all the elements opened wide—and let it soak for a few minutes. But be careful! Make sure the water has time to cool off a bit, and do not leave your knife soaking for too long or the plastic casing could melt. Remove the knife and scrub the joints with an old toothbrush to loosen the innermost specks of grime.

A simpler alternative: Put the dirty knife—again, fully opened—into your dishwasher.

In the field, try scouring your blade with ashes from the campfire.

REPAIRING COOKWARE

The bottom line is that there are not really many ways to field-repair cookware and utensils (these latter are small-ticket items anyway). If one of your cooking pots gets a dent, try gently hammering out the dent at home, using a rubber mallet. Remember to go slow and easy so as not to inflict even more damage on the poor malformed pot.

APPENDIX

Repair Facility Reference Guide

When the repair task seems too daunting or you just want the pros to handle it, try one of these well-respected repair shops.

Boulder Mountain Repair—bags, packs, tents, clothing
641 South Broadway
Boulder, CO 80305
(303) 499-3634

Dave Page, Cobbler—boots
3509 Evanston Avenue North
Seattle, WA 98103
(800) 252-1229
www.davepagecobbler.com

The Grant Boys—bags, packs, tents, stoves, lights, clothes
1750 Newport Boulevard
Costa Mesa, CA 92627
(949) 645-3400
www.grantboys.com

Kelso Camping and Repairs—bags, tents, clothes
P.O. Box 2714
Anaheim, CA 92804
(714) 827-7527
www.kelsocover.com

Needle Mountain Designs, Inc.—bags, packs, tents, clothes
P.O. Box 3578
Evergreen, CO 80437
(303) 674-2941, (303) 697-9396, or (720) 353-3128
NMDsewing@juno.com

Rainy Pass Repair, Inc.—bags, packs, tents, clothes
5307 Roosevelt Way Northeast
Seattle, WA 98105
(800) 747-7867
www.rainypass.com

Stitchlines—bags, packs, tents, clothes
3750 South Broadway
Englewood, CO 80110
(303) 781-9044

Sunshine Tent Pole Specialists—tent poles
23679 Calabasas Road, Suite 162
Calabasas, CA 91302
(818) 222-5217

TA Enterprises—tent poles
8212 Northeast 99th Circle
Vancouver, WA 98662
(800) 266-9527
www.polesforyou.com

Tent Repair Services—bags, packs, tents, clothes
20½ Sea Street
Camden, ME 04843
(207) 236-0997
tentrepair@acadia.net

ZRK Enterprises—bags, packs, tents
279 Palm Avenue, Suite 1
Ashland, OR 97520
(800) 735-4620
www.zipperrescue.com

THE MOUNTAINEERS, founded in 1906, is a nonprofit outdoor activity and conservation club, whose mission is "to explore, study, preserve, and enjoy the natural beauty of the outdoors. . . ." Based in Seattle, Washington, the club is now the third-largest such organization in the United States, with 15,000 members and five branches throughout Washington State.

The Mountaineers sponsors both classes and year-round outdoor activities in the Pacific Northwest, which include hiking, mountain climbing, ski-touring, snowshoeing, bicycling, camping, kayaking and canoeing, nature study, sailing, and adventure travel. The club's conservation division supports environmental causes through educational activities, sponsoring legislation, and presenting informational programs. All club activities are led by skilled, experienced volunteers, who are dedicated to promoting safe and responsible enjoyment and preservation of the outdoors.

If you would like to participate in these organized outdoor activities or the club's programs, consider a membership in The Mountaineers. For information and an application, write or call The Mountaineers, Club Headquarters, 300 Third Avenue West, Seattle, WA 98119; 206-284-6310.

The Mountaineers Books, an active, nonprofit publishing program of the club, produces guidebooks, instructional texts, historical works, natural history guides, and works on environmental conservation. All books produced by The Mountaineers Books fulfill the club's mission.

Send or call for our catalog of more than 500 outdoor titles:

The Mountaineers Books
1001 SW Klickitat Way, Suite 201
Seattle, WA 98134
800-553-4453
mbooks@mountaineersbooks.org
www.mountaineersbooks.org